W9-DGL-181

APOLLO'S FIRST
MOON LANDING

A FLY on the WALL HISTORY

BY THOMAS KINGSLEY TROUPE   ILLUSTRATED BY JOMIKE TEJIDO

PICTURE WINDOW BOOKS
a capstone imprint

Hi, I'm Horace, and this is my sister, Maggie.

We've been "flies on the wall" during important events in history.

We saw Johannes Gutenberg invent the printing press.

We saw Harriet Tubman escape from slavery.

We even watched more than 20,000 workers build the Taj Mahal!

Nothing could prepare us, though, for our out-of-this-world adventure in 1969 . . .

2

In the 1950s and 1960s, the whole world was excited about space travel. The United States and the Soviet Union had sent bugs, dogs, monkeys, and people into space. But no country had put a person on the moon yet. The United States wanted to be the first. To do that, they started the Apollo missions.

On July 16, 1969, Maggie and I were buzzing around Cape Canaveral, Florida. We saw a large group of people camped out. They all stared at a big metal tower in the distance.

Whoa, Maggie! Look at the size of that thing!

Is that some sort of jungle gym?

No, Horace, it's a launchpad for a rocket. A BIG rocket.

What are those crazy people up to now?

★ ★ ★

The *Apollo 11* / *Saturn V* rocket was the tallest of its time. At 363 feet (111 meters), it was about as tall as a 33-story building!

★ ★ ★

3

I had to get a better look, so Maggie and I flew to the tower. It stood at NASA's Kennedy Space Center. Near the top of the tower, we saw three men in puffy white jumpsuits. They wore helmets that looked like fish bowls. The men were astronauts. They walked toward a door on the side of the rocket.

The astronauts had their names on the front of their space suits: Armstrong, Aldrin, and Collins. They waved and climbed inside. I wanted to see what it looked like in there!

I think we better stay out here, Horace.

We don't want to BUG the astronauts.

Are you kidding? The one guy's nickname is "Buzz."

He'll love having us around!

＊＊＊

The astronauts on the Apollo 11 mission were Neil Armstrong, Michael Collins, and Edwin "Buzz" Aldrin.

4   ＊＊＊

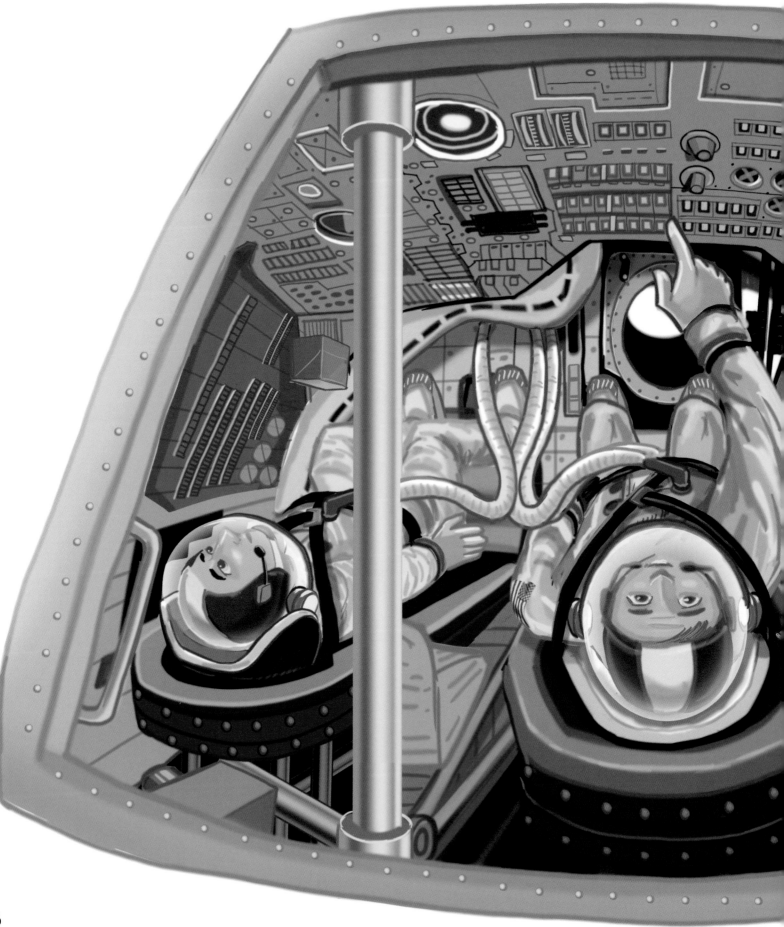

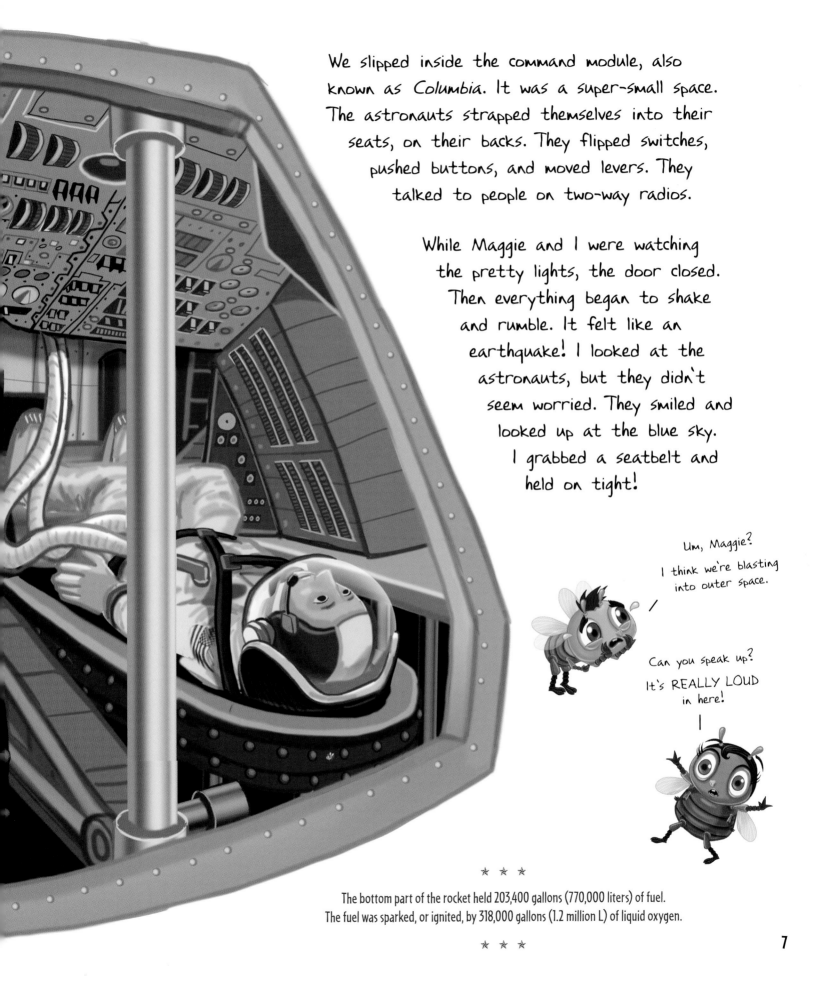

We slipped inside the command module, also known as Columbia. It was a super-small space. The astronauts strapped themselves into their seats, on their backs. They flipped switches, pushed buttons, and moved levers. They talked to people on two-way radios.

While Maggie and I were watching the pretty lights, the door closed. Then everything began to shake and rumble. It felt like an earthquake! I looked at the astronauts, but they didn't seem worried. They smiled and looked up at the blue sky. I grabbed a seatbelt and held on tight!

Um, Maggie?
I think we're blasting into outer space.

Can you speak up?
It's REALLY LOUD in here!

✫ ✫ ✫

The bottom part of the rocket held 203,400 gallons (770,000 liters) of fuel. The fuel was sparked, or ignited, by 318,000 gallons (1.2 million L) of liquid oxygen.

✫ ✫ ✫

LIFTOFF!

We zoomed straight into the sky.

After a while, parts of the rocket fell off! Crazy, right? The astronauts called the parts "stages."

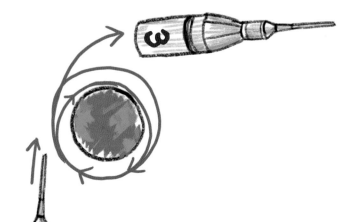

The rocket had three stages. Stages one and two fell off after their fuel burned up. Stage three shot us around Earth one and a half times. The planet looked like a bright blue marble.

After we circled Earth, the engines pushed us farther into space. We flew for a few days, and then, on July 19, Maggie and I finally saw where we were heading. The moon! We started orbiting it, and the astronauts got busy. Buzz and Neil checked on a special vehicle called the lunar module. They were going to fly it to the moon's surface.

It sure got quiet on the radio when we went behind the moon.

Yeah, all communication with Earth is cut off on the far side of the moon.

It's kind of scary for a few minutes, isn't it?

✳ ✳ ✳

Apollo 11 traveled 240,000 miles (386,243 kilometers) in 76 hours. That's as fast as going from New York City to Los Angeles, California, in about 53 minutes!

✳ ✳ ✳

The next day, Buzz and Neil said goodbye to Michael. They climbed out of the command module and strapped themselves into *Eagle* (that's what the astronauts called the lunar module). The hatch between the two modules closed.

Buzz and Neil pushed buttons and flipped switches. Then . . . . *BOOM!* *Eagle* unlocked from *Columbia*. And just like that, we were headed for the moon.

I can't believe they left Michael Collins behind.

Doesn't he want to go to the moon too?

I don't know.

Maybe he needs to stay with *Columbia* to make sure it doesn't fly away.

Ha! You mean, like WE'RE doing?

In our *EAGLE*?

＊ ＊ ＊

The astronauts called the team back on Earth "Houston."
NASA's mission control center was located in Houston, Texas.

＊ ＊ ＊

We glided away from Columbia. The moon's surface got closer and closer. Neil set us down gently, making sure we didn't land on any sharp rocks. He called back to Earth and said, "Houston, the Eagle has landed." We were by the Sea of Tranquility. But I didn't see any water. What kind of sea doesn't have water?

Neil and Buzz were pretty excited. They were supposed to take a nap for a few hours. Instead, they ate supper and talked to mission control. Then they put on their space suits. Maggie and I ducked inside Neil's helmet. We made sure to stay out of the way.

Are we really going out there? I heard the moon is made of cheese. It probably stinks.

That's not true, Horace! The moon isn't cheesy. Just dusty.

* * *

The Sea of Tranquility is a lunar mare. It's a sea on the moon.
But instead of holding water, it holds dark-gray rock called basalt.

* * *

Neil opened *Eagle's* door. The moon was bright and beautiful. As Neil climbed down the ladder, I saw it was a big step to the surface. That's when Neil said, "That's one small step for man, one giant leap for mankind." Then he hopped off the ladder and landed on the moon.

I can't believe we're here, Horace!

We're the first flies on the moon!

Hey, I think I can see our house from here!

★ ★ ★

Neil Armstrong turned on a camera as he climbed down the ladder. He used it to show the rest of the world his first steps on the moon.

★ ★ ★

14

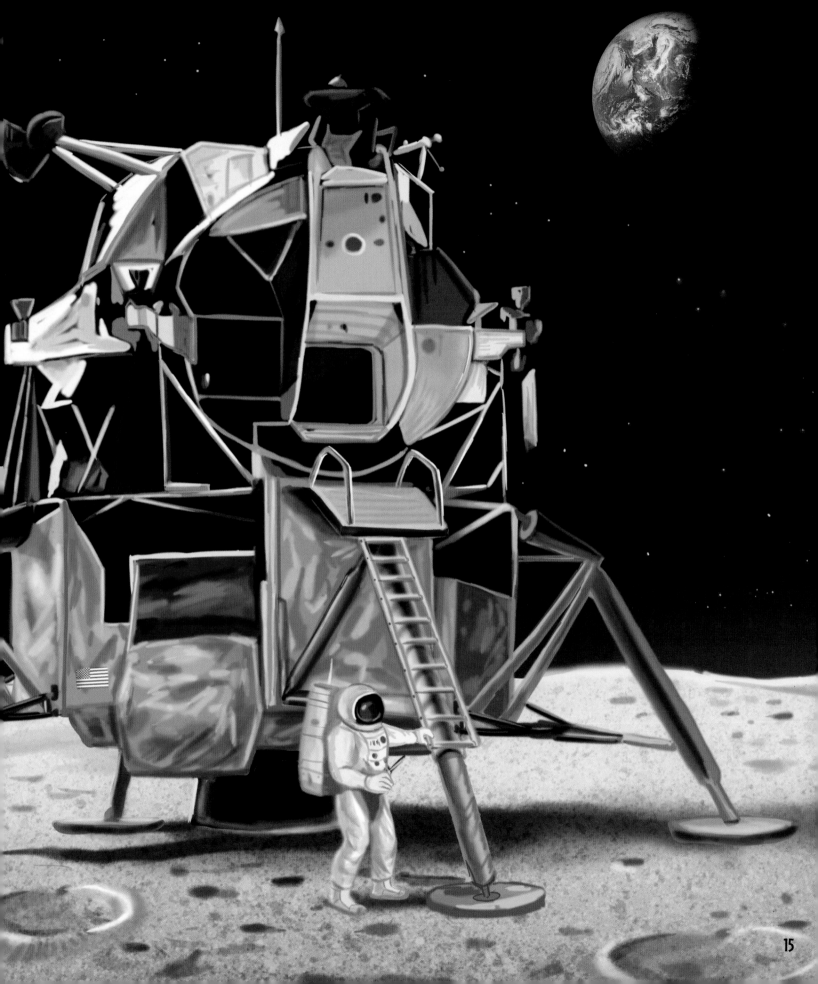

Then Buzz climbed out of the lunar module. He had to be careful closing the door. He didn't want to lock it by mistake!

Why does it feel so weird here on the lunar surface?

It's the gravity, Horace.

It's not as strong as it is on Earth. Everything here feels lighter.

✶ ✶ ✶

The moon's gravity is only 17 percent as strong as Earth's. For example, if you weigh 100 pounds (45 kilograms) on Earth, you would weigh 16 pounds (7 kg) on the moon.

✶ ✶ ✶

Both astronauts got to work quickly. They made sure Eagle wasn't damaged as it landed. They set up a U.S. flag. They took pictures and read from a sign they brought along. Everyone on Earth was super happy. President Richard Nixon even made a phone call to Neil and Buzz.

Neil and Buzz hopped around the moon. Neil picked up some moon rocks. Buzz kicked dust. They took lots of pictures. They also set up some scientific equipment. One of the machines measured the amount of energy coming from the sun. Another measured the distance between the moon and Earth.

In addition to moon rocks, the astronauts took core samples. They used tubes to pull material from 5 inches (13 centimeters) below the moon's surface.

One of these machines measures earthquakes.

Um, wouldn't that be MOONquakes, Maggie?

Very funny, Horace. Very funny . . .

We were having a lot of fun, but soon it was time to leave. Maggie thought Michael Collins might be lonely floating around in *Columbia* by himself. Neil had walked on the moon for two and a half hours. Buzz had walked a little less than two hours.

Neil and Buzz said goodbye to the moon and climbed back inside the lunar module. When they took off their helmets, they wrinkled their noses. They talked about how stinky their space suits were. After that, they rested.

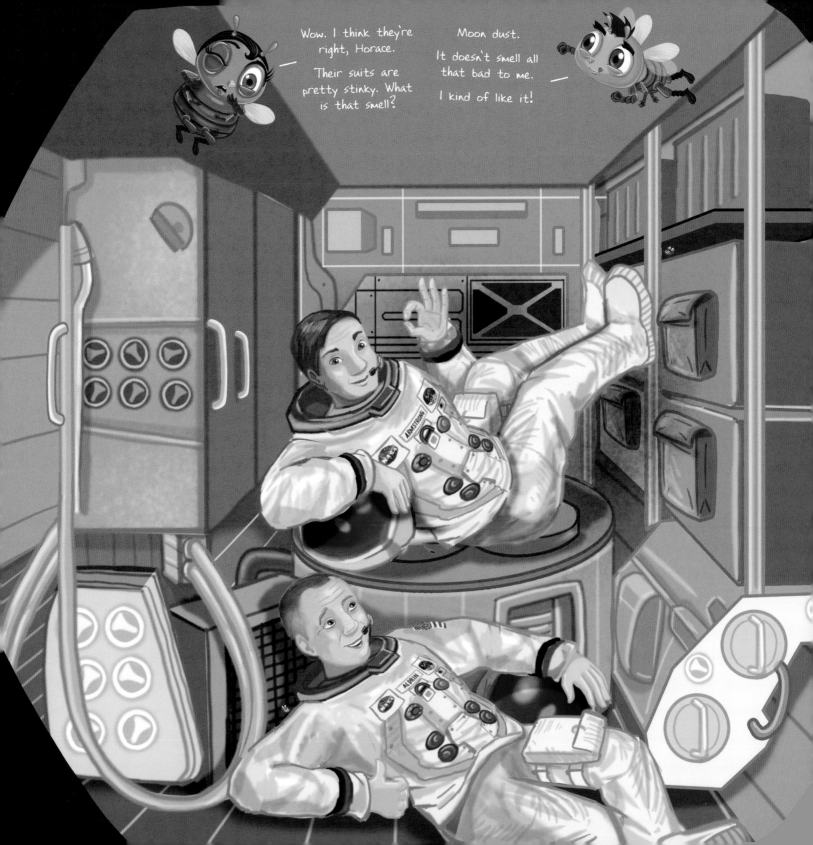

When the astronauts woke up, it was time to blast off. We needed to fly back to *Columbia* — and then back to Earth. *Eagle* took off, leaving its landing legs on the moon.

I'm glad they left part of the lunar module behind.

I'm not a big fan of eagles.

Yeah, but they're leaving a lot of stuff behind.

Neil steered carefully. It took a few tries, but he got us reconnected with *Columbia*. All three astronauts were together again.

Neil and Buzz moved all the samples they had collected into *Columbia*. And then, a few hours later, they cut *Eagle* loose . . .

and it floated away into space.

★ ★ ★

No one knows for sure what happened to the lunar module after it was cut loose.
Scientists believe *Eagle* orbited the moon for one to four months before finally crashing into it.

★ ★ ★

Maggie and I watched the astronauts get ready for the journey back home. They aimed for Earth and blasted off.

One of the astronauts said it would take about 60 hours to get there. Sixty hours! We'd been in space a long time already!

As we got close to Earth, our final engine burned up its fuel and dropped off. All that was left was *Columbia*, the command module. We zoomed toward our home planet.

Is it me, or did it get hot in here, Maggie?

I think *Columbia* is on fire!

You're right, Horace!

Chunks of it are flying off too!

* * *

Columbia was designed to withstand incredible fire and heat. The covering kept the astronauts inside safe, although bits of the heat shield did come off.

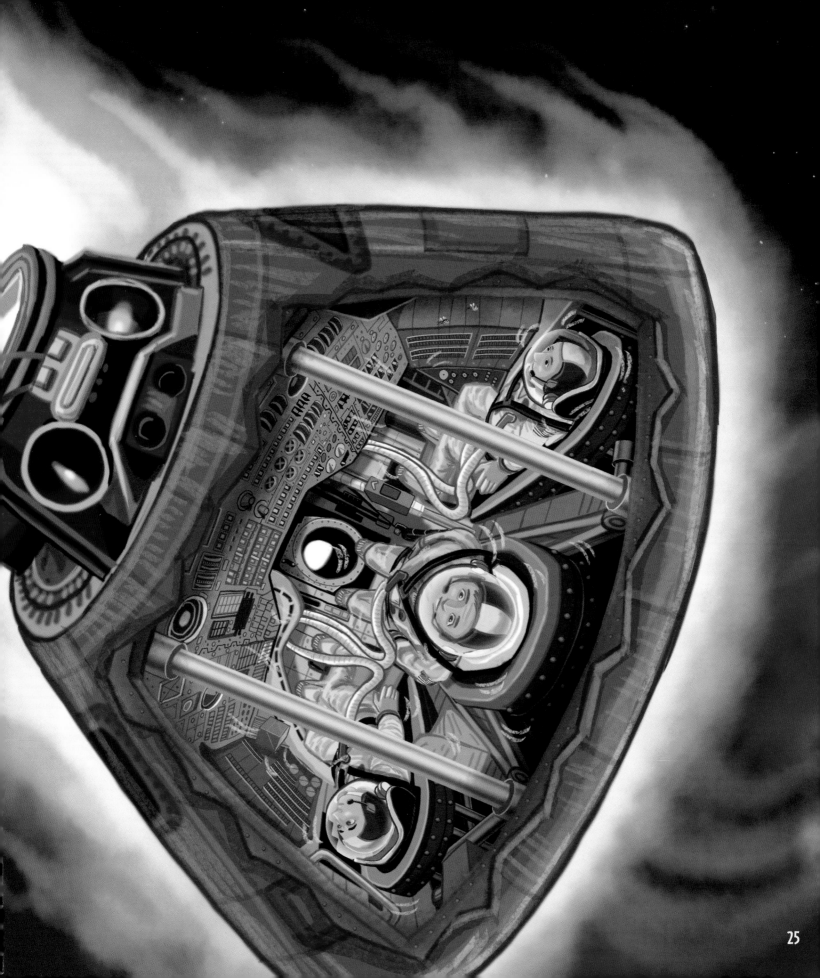

Maggie, the astronauts, and I were coming in incredibly fast! Then three colorful parachutes popped out of Columbia to slow us down. We all caught our breath as we drifted gently down to Earth.

SPLASH! We landed in the Pacific Ocean. Maggie was worried she'd get seasick. But the astronauts were happy, we were home, and the mission was a success!

I don't feel so good, Horace.

I really hope we didn't get all the way back home just to sink in the ocean.

Don't worry, sis.

I hear helicopters. Help is on the way!

Boy, it sure feels good to be home, doesn't it?

HORNET + 3

After the astronauts came back to Earth, they were quarantined.
They had to stay by themselves in a special trailer for three weeks.
Doctors wanted to make sure the astronauts hadn't brought
home any diseases from the moon.

★ ★ ★

The Apollo 11 astronauts were seen as heroes. They had made the American dream of visiting the moon come true.

NASA continued with the Apollo program, sending astronauts to the moon five more times. The Apollo 15 mission was the first to send a wheeled vehicle to the lunar surface. The Apollo Lunar Roving Vehicle could carry one or two astronauts.

The last time NASA sent a crew to the moon was the Apollo 17 mission. The United States hasn't been back since December of 1972.

TIMELINE

NOVEMBER 3, 1957
The Soviet Union launches *Sputnik 2,* with the first living passenger aboard – a dog named Laika.

MAY 28, 1959
The United States launches the first successful space mission with primates aboard. The monkeys' names are Able and Baker.

MAY 25, 1961
President John F. Kennedy makes a bold proposal. He says that, before 1970, the United States should commit itself to putting an American on the moon and returning him safely.

APRIL 12, 1961
Soviet cosmonaut Yuri Gagarin becomes the first man in space, with a 108-minute flight on *Vostok 1.*

FEBRUARY 20, 1962
John Glenn makes the first U.S. manned orbital flight aboard *Mercury 6.*

MAY 14, 1973
A *Saturn V* rocket launches Skylab, the United States' first space station.

AUGUST 20, 1977
The space probe *Voyager 2* is launched toward the planets Uranus and Neptune.

JULY 20, 1969
Six years after John F. Kennedy's death, the Apollo 11 crew lands on the moon. They fulfill his goal set in 1961.

SEPTEMBER 5, 1977
Voyager 1 is launched to perform flybys of the planets Jupiter and Saturn.

APRIL 12, 1981
The space shuttle *Columbia* lifts off from Cape Canaveral, Florida. The first space mission for NASA's new astronaut transportation system begins.

GLOSSARY

Apollo–a Greek and Roman god; all U.S. space missions to the moon were named after Apollo

astronaut–a space pilot or traveler

cosmonaut–an astronaut from the Soviet Union

gravity–a force that pulls objects with mass together

launchpad–a large area where a spacecraft is loaded and blasts off into space

lunar–having to do with a moon

mare–a large, fairly flat dark area on the moon; *mare* is the Latin word for "sea"

mission–a planned job or task

module–a self-contained unit that can work by itself but is also part of a larger spacecraft

NASA–a U.S. government agency that runs the space program; abbreviation for National Aeronautics and Space Administration

orbit–to travel around an object in space

quarantine–to keep a person, animal, or plant away from others to stop a disease from spreading

Soviet Union–a former federation of 15 republics that included Russia, Ukraine, and other nations of eastern Europe and northern Asia

stage–part of a rocket that holds fuel and engines

THINK ABOUT IT

1. Why do you think the astronauts were strapped into their seats on their backs, instead of sitting up, during liftoff? Use the illustrations on pages 6 to 8 to explain your answer.

2. Describe the steps Neil Armstrong and Edwin "Buzz" Aldrin took to travel from the command module to the moon's suface.

3. Explain what Neil Armstrong meant when he said, "That's one small step for man, one giant leap for mankind."

READ MORE

Aguilar, David A. *Space Encyclopedia: A Tour of Our Solar System and Beyond.* Washington, D.C.: National Geographic, 2013.

Snedden, Robert. *A Brief Illustrated History of Space Exploration.* Mankato, Minn.: Capstone Publishing, 2017.

Yomtov, Nel. *The Apollo 11 Moon Landing: July 20, 1969.* Mankato, Minn.: Capstone Publishing, 2014.

INTERNET SITES

Use FactHound to find Internet sites related to this book:

Visit *www.facthound.com*

Just type in 9781515815983 and go.

Check out projects, games and lots more at
www.capstonekids.com

INDEX

Look for other books in the series:

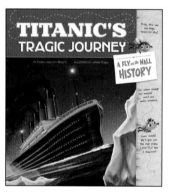

Special thanks to our adviser, Kevin Byrne, PhD, Professor Emeritus of History, Gustavus Adolphus College, for his expertise.

Picture Window Books is published by Capstone,
1710 Roe Crest Drive, North Mankato, Minnesota 56003
www.mycapstone.com

Library of Congress Cataloging-in-Publication data is available on the Library of Congress website.
ISBN 978-1-5158-1598-3 (library binding)
ISBN 978-1-5158-1602-7 (paperback)
ISBN 978-1-5158-1606-5 (eBook PDF)

Summary: Describes the events leading up to and including the Apollo 11 moon landing with Neil Armstrong, Michael Collins, and Edwin "Buzz" Aldrin.

Editor: Jill Kalz
Designer: Sarah Bennett
Creative Director: Nathan Gassman
Production Specialist: Laura Manthe

The illustrations in this book were planned with pencil on paper and finished with digital paints.

Printed and bound in the United States of America.
010850S18